THE LAST SERMON

THE LAST SERMON

M. J. Deschamps

All Scripture quotations are from the NEW AMERICAN STANDARD BIBLE®, Copyright © 1960, 1962, 1963, 1968, 1971, 1972, 1973, 1975, 1977, 1995 by The Lockman Foundation. Used by permission.

Copyright © 2023 Michael Deschamps.

All rights reserved. No part of this publication may be reproduced, distributed, or transmitted in any form or by any means, including photocopying, recording, or other electronic or mechanical methods, without the prior written permission of the publisher, except in the case of brief quotations embodied in critical reviews and certain other noncommercial uses permitted by copyright law. For permission requests, write to the publisher, addressed "Attention: Permissions Coordinator," at the email address below.

ISBN: 979-8-218-32465-0 (Paperback)
Library of Congress Control Number: 2023924281
First printing edition 2023.

TheLastSermon1@Gmail.com

*This book is dedicated to my wife of forty-something
years, Linda, and to my beloved children, Laura,
Kimberly, Matthew, Elizabeth, and Hannah
who have enriched my life beyond measure.*

PREFACE

Behold, days are coming,
declares the Lord God,
When I will send a famine on the land.
Not a famine for bread or a thirst for water,
but rather for hearing
the words of the Lord.

AMOS 8:11

My purpose for writing this book is simple: my heart is burdened for this generation of souls living today. We have more than any other previous generation, yet we have lost much more. In this fast paced, technologically advanced world we live in, I fear we are failing to recognize what is truly important.

Now that I am in my latter years, my perspective encompasses looking back as well as looking forward. Much more than longing for the "good old days," I believe there is a dire need to *carpe diem* (seize the day). But how do we do that? We are all so busy with the here and now. However, the here and now is by its very nature very temporal, so how do we shift our focus to the big picture?

I am thankful to have been raised in a loving, but not perfect, family. Then started a loving, but not perfect, family of my own. Through all of this, the importance I placed on the subject of God ebbed and flowed, but He didn't. I was raised in one Christian denomination, then explored several others, then enrolled in seminary, then pastored small fellowships. Through it all, I discovered that no human institution is perfect, but God is. The ultimate need for Him has never changed but has become more obscure with the many distractions that abound. I believe it is imperative to understand the nature of these "distractions," their root cause, why they are so dangerous, and what to do about them.

None of us knows which is our last day here on this earth. None of us knows which is the last sermon we will hear. But we do have this day.

CONTENTS

Preface 7

Introduction 11

1. The Last Sermon 17

2. The Reckoning 23

3. The Here and Now 27

4. The Word 35

5. The Most Important Question 43

6. Salvation 57

7. The Church 73

8. The World 89

INTRODUCTION

We are living in our last days—everyone reading this will most likely cross the threshold into eternal life within the next fifty years or so. Some will pass much sooner, and a few others may last a bit longer. There are no guarantees that tomorrow will come for all of us. With this fact in mind, I thought that a review of the last sermon I think we will ever hear would be appropriate. I am referring to the sermon Jesus will preach when He pulls all of us together at the judgment and separates the goats from the sheep. Read in context, this judgment (the sheep and goats) happens just after Jesus' second coming, immediately after the great tribulation (Matt. 25:19, 31–33). The *final* (great white throne) judgment happens *after* Jesus' 1,000-year reign on earth (Rev. 20:7–15).

When Jesus addresses the masses on judgment day, there seems to be some confusion among the listeners. I want to try and clarify some important things so that, in the end, the end we all will face, there will be less confusion. Once we arrive at that moment in time, there will be no reprieve, no going back, no mulligans, defenses, compromise, tolerance, or debate. We will find ourselves on either the right or the left of Jesus with no further opportunities to change our fate. Because this date with destiny is inescapable for mankind. For anyone professing to be Christian, I wanted to clarify a few things in the hope that when we arrive there, there will be fewer surprises.

The concern is that there are people running around thinking they are Christians but are not. This becomes obvious in what Jesus says at the judgment. The only way to heaven is through salvation, and Satan's greatest deception is to lull us into a false sense of security regarding our salvation. He gets people to believe that because they said a phrase, or invited the Lord into their heart, or said a prayer that they have been born again. But they may not in fact have experienced the new birth. Unfortunately, many of these people continue with their lives until that fateful day when they cross over and find themselves corralled with the goats, perplexed, and confused.

So how can we be certain of our standing? As professing Christians, we are told to work out our salvation with fear and trembling. Paul says to the Philippians:

> So then, my beloved, just as you have always obeyed, not as in my presence only, but now much more in my absence, *work out your salvation*

> *with fear and trembling; for it is God who is at work in you, both to will and to work for His good pleasure.*[1]

My hope in writing this book is to help the reader to understand what this means and to alert the professing Christian to the false realities of Satan. I quote a good deal of Scripture, but I advise everyone to verify the verses themselves with prayer and study.

The Word of God, the Bible, is the spring from which all truth comes and the platform upon which all truth is measured, tested, and confirmed. If you do believe in God's Word as delivered in the Bible, then you will need to keep it close at hand as a guide to help you examine your faith. The Bible is where we learn of God, His purpose, and His will.

"Am I saved? Am I really born again of the Spirit of God?" Many professing Christians claim this but know little about it. What we see in today's world is a *visible church*, a broken and divided reality. There is nothing more revealing about the true state of our salvation than to have a good look at how we fit into today's world.

---

1. Philippians 2:12–14. Emphasis mine

1
THE LAST SERMON

I crested the hill and for as far as I could see there were millions and millions of people standing, shifting, but eerily silent. Their faces reflected a host of emotions, everything from awe to guilt to stern confidence. The sky was a stale blue and the ground, what I could see of it between the feet of the people, was a dusty pale green. It was an eerie daylight caught somewhere between dusk and dawn. Everyone was facing one direction. I followed their gaze to a hilltop perch where *He* was standing. He was silent and still. His hair was long and tangled with His brown beard. He stared out at the multitude of onlookers and, portraying a sense of formidable reckoning, began to speak:

> But when the Son of Man comes in His glory, and all the angels with Him, then He will sit on His glorious throne. All the nations will be gathered before Him; and He will separate them from one another, as the shepherd separates the sheep from the goats; and He will put the sheep on His right, and the goats on the left.

Then the King will say to those on His right, "Come, you who are blessed of My Father, inherit the kingdom prepared for you from the foundation of the world. For I was hungry, and you gave Me something to eat; I was thirsty, and you gave Me something to drink; I was a stranger, and you invited Me in; naked, and you clothed Me; I was sick, and you visited Me; I was in prison, and you came to Me." Then the righteous will answer Him, "Lord, when did we see You hungry, and feed You, or thirsty, and give You something to drink? And when did we see You a stranger, and invite You in, or naked, and clothe You? When did we see You sick, or in prison, and come to You?" The King will answer and say to them, "Truly I say to you, to the extent that you did it to one of these brothers of Mine, even the least of them, you did it to Me."

Then He will also say to those on His left, "Depart from Me, accursed ones, into the eternal fire which has been prepared for the devil and his angels; for I was hungry, and you gave Me nothing to eat; I was thirsty, and you gave Me nothing to drink; I was a stranger, and you did not invite Me in; naked, and you did not clothe Me; sick, and in prison, and you did not visit Me." Then they themselves also will answer, "Lord, when did we see You hungry, or thirsty, or a stranger, or naked, or sick, or in prison, and did not take

> care of You?" Then He will answer them, "Truly
> I say to you, to the extent that you did not do it
> to one of the least of these, you did not do it to
> Me." These will go away into eternal punishment,
> but the righteous into eternal life.[2]

He then simply turned away and vanished. The crowd stirred, looking at one another in dismay, some in confusion and others in angst, and still others taking defensive postures. Many were reaching toward the now vacant perch and mumbling things I could not hear. Then suddenly the ground began to shift, and a wall appeared in the middle of the multitude. It grew skyward, higher and higher until it was unscalable. I began to hear murmuring and anxious talk blurred into a thousand voices. A strange sight caught my attention when I noticed the opposing sides of the crowd divided by the high wall. Facing the people from the same vantage point as He had when He spoke, I saw a huge number segregated to the left side of the wall and a much smaller multitude gathered on the right. These verses came to mind: "Many are called but few are chosen"[3] and "Enter through the narrow gate; for the gate is wide and the way is broad that leads to destruction, and there are many who enter through it. For the gate is small and the way is narrow that leads to life, and there are few who find it."[4]

---

2. Matthew 25:31–46.

3. Matthew 22:14.

4. Matthew 7:13–14.

Then the crowds simply vanished, followed by a sudden and deafening silence. Time and opportunity gone forever—in a millisecond.

2

THE RECKONING

For we must all appear before the judgment seat of Christ, so that each one may be recompensed for his deeds in the body, according to what he has done, whether good or bad.

2 CORINTHIANS 5:12.

I could not erase that scene nor those faces from my mind. "It is coming," I thought. "It is nearer than we imagine." There has been so much clamoring about the end times, the rapture, the escape routes so many of us embrace as a near-term hope to all our problems. We have been enamored with a great deal of detail and attention regarding that epic drama of the last days. We may well be moving toward that final chapter in the story of mankind, that drama laid open for centuries about the return of Jesus. The amount of attention made by so many generations awaiting the return of our Savior to judge the world seems to have derailed many of us from embracing our day-to-day living in Christ. That cleverly constructed distraction may have stolen from the masses the scant time they have left on the earth to ensure their salvation and place in heaven. These are the exploits of that genius fallen angel, Satan, that have captured so many. Each of us is always living in our last days. Yes, Jesus will return, but on His timeline. Death comes to each of us within a single lifetime. For some very unexpectantly and quickly.

One day at a time is all we are allotted. Each morning we wake up we should count as a blessing because tomorrow is never guaranteed. Today is the final day for thousands. It will one day be ours as well.

It became painfully apparent to me that once that fateful day arrives, all future opportunity will be lost. Once we face that judgment, there will be no opportunity for salvation or repentance. We will be mute. That reckoning, for many, will hit like a blacksmith's hammer, crashing loudly on the anvil of judgment. This is our future, and no one can escape it.

3

THE HERE AND NOW

Your gold and your silver have rusted; and their rust will be a witness against you and will consume your flesh like fire. It is in the last days that you have stored up your treasure!

JAMES 5:3

This is the place where we all live right now, in the here and now. It is a gaping slot for change and opportunity. But it does not last long. And the cares of this world and the pursuits of our lives make it pass by lightning fast. At the end of our here and now we all have a date with judgment. That is our inescapable future. We do have the priceless gift of time in the present, a gift of time to learn the truth and a gift of choice and of change. This is our opportunity to find our place in God's world.

We only have today. Maybe tomorrow. Maybe a thousand tomorrows, but none are guaranteed. Depressing? Maybe to some, but every day is a chance to begin anew, refreshed, confident in our salvation and place on the right side of that eternal wall. Clever Satan has created for us perpetual distractions and *meaningful* plans to entangle us in the cares of this world. Yes, plan for your retirement. It may come. But first plan for your eternity, which is guaranteed, and of much longer duration.

So, what do we do? Taking a long, hard look at reality is a starting point. A planet full of nature and full of people. Hanging in space, surrounded by the inexplicable beauty of the universe. Most of us are so busy with life we miss a great deal of what is eternally important. But that is the devil's plan: to busy every soul into eternal damnation. To placate us with a false purpose, a false reality, and a false understanding that separates us from our loving Father. Satan is the father of lies[5] and his created realities are alluring and treacherous. Many of us are caught up in them, busy trying to better our temporal, short lives at the inestimable cost of our eternal souls. Why? Because somewhere along the road we got diverted by an enticing lie, having our ego or lust caught in a snare, twisted by misleading assumptions, manufactured pretenses mingled with our own selfish motives.

Christianity and salvation exist only in God's reality. What that means is that the first step is to see our reality for what it truly is: God's reality, not man's. From the beginning was the Word.[6] God created our entire world, our present reality, from nothing and with a distinct and divine purpose.[7] He created us man and woman for His good pleasure, equipping us for eternal life in His glorious presence. Then Satan entered the scene and exploited the pride, ego, and lust of mankind, and sin entered the world. Sin stays in the world.

---

5. John 8:24.

6. John 1:1–4.

7. Genesis 1, 2.

Sin is active and rampant in our reality—a fallen reality. Sin causes eternal death to our souls. Then the loving Father steps in to negate the just consequences of sin by offering His only Son, to take on flesh and become a man, and be crucified by His own creation. The pathway to eternal salvation is in place, not by our engineering prowess or works, but by the love of God. A free and eternal offering. A real and necessary offering if any human is to escape the sentence of hell. That is our reality.

If we fail to realize that only one reality exists, God's, then we have been deceived for the sole purpose of our destruction. The enemy has twisted mankind's perception to imagine hundreds of possible realities, all in opposition to God's, and many reasonably constructed and very welcoming. Apart from God's reality the idea of salvation is pointless. If we do not see, understand, and embrace God's reality as the only reality, we are doomed to deception. We need to be able to distinguish the Father's plan from the multitude of enticing fakes created by the enemy. The created world has been given to Satan to do with what he pleases. Which means that what we see in the flesh, and what we perceive as countless realms of enticing possibilities, are only false holographic traps to lure us away from God's reality.

So, how can we tell the difference between God's reality and the free and alluring false realities of the devil? The Bible. The Word. The truth. It's all in there somewhere. The past few generations have had the immense blessing of having the written

Word readily available. Our generation has even more access to the Bible and to serious study because of the internet and the modern tools of the computer, huge storage drives, and easy access to billions of pages of recorded history, commentaries, and Bible teachings. No one from our generation will be able to stand before the Lord in judgment and say, "We didn't know." These tools are available and easily reachable. The truth is out there. There will be no excuses as to why we never cared to find it.

It can be difficult to navigate spiritual life in a fallen world. Dietrich Bonhoeffer defined it best when he described fallen man's noble efforts to right a fallen reality, but this is a fallen world, and it can never be transformed by fallen means.[8] All effort and hope in this fallen world outside the reality of God are hopeless. This is easy to see in the endless efforts of goodwill and yet the continued downward spiraling of our world. All attempts at neutralizing the devastating effects of sin on our world, however sprung from good motives, are useless endeavors. Man, apart from God, will never right this fallen world. Never. All hope of fixing this place apart from God are empty. Satan has done an excellent job of removing God from our daily lives. All politically proposed solutions to the growing problems in our world are devoid of God. We have rejected God's reality for our own. We have traded eternal life for noble pursuits of happiness that just make us feel better. Every day we are led further astray. Every

---

8. D. Bonhoeffer, *Ethics*, New York, NY, Touchstone Press, Simon & Schuster, 1995.

day we lose another opportunity to repent and return to our heavenly Father.

We must acknowledge God's reality. We must learn of Him, His will, and His purpose from Bible study and fellowship. We must learn about salvation and eternal life. We must embrace and hold fast to the truth. There is nothing as meaningful and fulfilling as the knowledge of God and His will. Most everyone reading this probably has a Bible. But how many of us have read it with purpose? How many of us have read it more than once? We must understand that salvation is predicated upon God's reality, knowledge of Him, His will, and His divine purpose—His salvation. We start with the Word of God. We believe it and embrace it. There is no other way.

4

THE WORD

Thy word is a lamp unto my feet,
And a light unto my path.
I have sworn, and have confirmed it,
That I will observe thy righteous ordinances.

PSALM 119:105–106

No one who stands before the Lord at judgment will suffer loss because they believed in and adhered to the Word of God. Many may fall by the wayside saying that they listened to this teacher or that preacher, taking their spoken word as gospel and never thinking to verify what they heard. The Bible is there for us to utilize as a guide, a "lamp" to our feet, a guiding light to the right path in our complex and busy life. As Christians it is our responsibility to learn and grow according to God's will. The Bible is the Word of God, and we must study it if we are to navigate successfully through Satan's hall of mirrors.

Going to church and hearing sermon after sermon is simply not enough. It's certainly easier than digging in and studying the Bible on our own, but it is not a guaranteed means to the truth. About 31 percent of the world's population is considered to be Christian. There are believed to be more than 40,000 Christian denominations around the world and over 200 in the United States alone.[9] If every Christian embraced

---

9. Kamila Klein, "*The Ultimate Guide: How Many Christian Denominations Are There in the World?*" Christianeducatorsacademy.com, 10-01-2023

the truth, there would be no denominations. What a thought! When we study church history, we see that all church splits were the result of differing opinions of what the Bible says. Our generation has always had the tools available to find and study God's Word. But the question will be, did we use them to the greatest extent to inform our beliefs and confirm our salvation?

Luke records in the book of Acts that the Berean Jews were more noble than the Jews in Thessalonica: "Now these were more noble than those in Thessalonica, in that they received the word with all readiness of mind, examining the scriptures daily, whether these things were so."[10] They were more noble not because they heard the Word of God with great excitement and expectation, but because they went *daily* to the Scriptures to verify the spoken words with the written Word. What we hear may sound good, but we must examine what we hear with the Bible.

This understanding is critical to what is to follow, because as Christians we acknowledge God's Word as the sole source of truth by which we are held accountable. The Bible sheds light on everything. Paul admonishes Timothy to use the Word and hold fast to God's Word and we must do the same:

> I solemnly charge you in the presence of God and of Christ Jesus, who is to judge the living and the dead, and by His appearing and His

---

10. Acts 17:11.

> kingdom: preach the word; be ready in season and out of season; reprove, rebuke, exhort, with great patience and instruction. *For the time will come when they will not endure sound doctrine; but wanting to have their ears tickled, they will accumulate for themselves teachers in accordance to their own desires and will turn away their ears from the truth and will turn aside to myths.*[11]

We have arrived at this point in history. It is a treacherous and evil time. Much of the truth has been ignored by modern Christianity. Over 40,000 Christian denominations permeate the globe because of deception and ignorance. There are pieces of God's truth embedded in all these false realities. Can we tell the difference? Which one are we a part of and why are we a part of it? Are we confident enough in our actuality to wager the eternal state of our souls?

Digging deep into the Bible will take effort. It is an exercise in self-reflection that disallows shallow facades. There is nothing to hide behind when we go to the Word to find the truth. Many fail to do so because they believe ignorance will give them pardon during the judgment. "Ignorance is bliss" is short lived. Some do so because they choose ignorance as permission to live lifestyles they know are in direct conflict to God's will. Willful neglect of God's Word will only further condemn us at the judgment. Our world is the way it

---

11. 2 Timothy 4:1–4. Emphasis mine.

is today because the truth of God's Word has been willfully and conveniently ignored.

Christianity is not a fad or a fashion. Christianity, in its true form, is God's genuineness in the flesh. There are many people who call themselves Christians who may find themselves on the wrong side of that wall at the judgment. We want to avoid that at all costs! Salvation belongs only to the true Christian.

> But realize this, that in the last days difficult times will come. For men will be lovers of self, lovers of money, boastful, arrogant, revilers, disobedient to parents, ungrateful, unholy, unloving, irreconcilable, malicious gossips, without self-control, brutal, haters of good, treacherous, reckless, conceited, lovers of pleasure rather than lovers of God, holding to a form of godliness, although they have denied its power; Avoid such men as these. For among them are those who enter into households and captivate weak women weighed down with sins, led on by various impulses, always learning and never able to come to the knowledge of the truth.[12]

The visible church encompasses persons who claim to be Christian and the "churches" that round them up every week. There are true believers in that mix. This visible church has a

---

12. 2 Timothy 3:1–7.

form of godliness but no real power, no spiritual power evident because they have denied the truth. We must accept the fact that the world is full of confessing Christians, but many may be deceived regarding their true state. We have thousands of visible churches and yet they have little or no spiritual power because they have rejected the truth and have led many unsuspecting people astray. The solution is for everyone to work out their own salvation, and that can be done only by knowing and studying God's Word. The only thing that sets us apart in the end is whether we are truly saved. The burden for that search rests only on you and me as confessing believers.

The work of Satan is remarkable. He lives only to destroy and twist everything God holds dear into unrecognizable, but attractive, filth and decay. Immensely skillful and persistent at turning everything from good to evil, he is a master at this game. It takes a thorough knowledge of God's Word to counteract his deceptions. He cares nothing for anyone. He does not care about the billions of people who do not confess Christ: they are already his. Instead, he spends every second of his existence trying to deceive and destroy Christians. He is ruthless yet very subtle. He is focused and masterful at long-term planning. He can be disguised as an angel of light. He spoils the purity of absolute white by having put in one drop of blackness at a time over centuries. What we think we see as white is only grey; we just have difficulty discerning the changes because some of us have no idea what pure white looks like:

> For the mystery of lawlessness is already at work; only he who now restrains will do so until he is taken out of the way. Then that lawless one will be revealed whom the Lord will slay with the breath of His mouth and bring to an end by the appearance of His coming; that is, the one whose coming is in accord with the activity of Satan, with all power and signs and false wonders, and with all the deception of wickedness *for those who perish, because they did not receive the love of the truth so as to be saved. For this reason God will send upon them a deluding influence so that they will believe what is false, in order that they all may be judged who did not believe the truth but took pleasure in wickedness.*[13]

The love of the truth saves. True believers possess this love, but imposters do not. This leads to another sobering truth: only true believers can see the truth. The Bible is the source for true believers to find their way through this world. True Christians embrace the Word of God—they grip it tight. It nourishes their soul. Some of us may need a realignment to God's reality and His purposes. If you have doubts about your salvation, then what is to come should help you discern your true state.

---

13. 2 Thessalonians 2:7–12. Emphasis mine.

5

THE MOST IMPORTANT QUESTION

That which is born of the flesh is flesh, and that which is born of the Spirit is spirit. Do not be amazed that I said to you, 'You must be born again'.

JOHN 3:6,7

What is a Christian? This is a serious question and one where the answer may appear to be simple. It is not. The construct of Christianity within God's reality is this: a Christian is a person who believes in Jesus Christ as the Son of God *because* they have been born again by the Spirit of God. What does this mean? Referring entirely to persons of the age of reason who have a working mind, freedom of choice, and the ability to find and know the truth, no one who has not been born again is a Christian. Going forward, only the title "Christian" will be used, because either one is, or is not, a Christian. The following explanation of the parable of the Sower demonstrates how some who may consider themselves Christian actually fall away over time.

> Now the parable is this: The seed is the word of God. And those by the wayside are they that have heard; then comes the devil, and takes away the word from their heart, that they may not believe

and be saved. And those on the rock are they who, when they have heard, receive the word with joy; and these have no root, who for a while believe, and in time of temptation fall away. And that which fell among the thorns, these are they that have heard, and as they go on their way they are choked with cares and riches and pleasures of this life and bring no fruit to perfection. And that in the good ground, these are such as in an honest and good heart, having heard the word, hold it fast, and bring forth fruit with patience.[14]

The Word of God is plentiful. It is the catalyst to salvation. It spurs the heart of the true believer. If the Word of God does not stir your heart, then salvation may be lacking. When Jesus was casting out a demon, the Pharisees made a ridiculous statement. Jesus answered them with a decisive argument that will help us better understand the relationship between a true believer and the Word of God:

> And He was casting out a demon, and it was mute; when the demon had gone out, the mute man spoke; and the crowds were amazed. But some of them said, "He casts out demons by Beelzebul, the ruler of the demons." Others, to test Him, were demanding of Him a sign from heaven. But He knew their thoughts and said to

---

14. Luke 8:11–15.

them, "Any kingdom divided against itself is laid waste; and a house divided against itself falls. If Satan also is divided against himself, how will his kingdom stand? For you say that I cast out demons by Beelzebul. And if I by Beelzebul cast out demons, by whom do your sons cast them out? So, they will be your judges. But if I cast out demons by the finger of God, then the kingdom of God has come upon you."[15]

If Satan's kingdom cannot be divided against itself and survive, neither can the kingdom of God be divided. Therefore, the true believer cannot be in opposition to God's Word. The Christian cannot both agree with some of God's Word and reject some of it. The Christian cannot redefine God's Word to suit their lifestyle or to make their reality more palatable. To claim to be a Christian and not to believe and embrace *all* of God's Word is a contradiction. It would be divisive. In God's design the true believer and God's Word are inseparable.

Always remember that Satan is *the* master deceiver. His mission, if he cannot get a person to reject God's reality, is to instill doubt and confusion. Many people say that there are contradictions and errors in the Bible. Satan's argument is that if the Bible is not perfect it cannot be God's Word because God is perfect. God is perfect; men are not. This is one reason there are over 40,000 Christian denominations across

---

15. Luke 11:14–20.

the world. The devil has championed a battle against God's Word since the Garden of Eden. He has been victorious in many ways. For example, if we were to go to a Christian book site and look up "Bible" we would be inundated with hundreds of options. There are Bibles for every age, every situation, and seemingly every mood. It is especially difficult for a new believer to know what a solid Bible looks like. Some are written in old English, like the King James Bible. Others are rewritten to make the language more modern, like the New King James Bible or the New International Version. Some of these efforts are noble and have helped believers to find a Bible that is easier to read. But being easy to read should not mean that it softens its edges regarding God's Word. Many efforts at marketing different versions of the Bible have diluted the Word of God. Many study Bibles are written by scholars who adhere to a specific belief or theological perspective, and their version of the Bible is written in support of their perspective. Satan has watered down the church and the Word of God to cater to the welcoming arms of many who want to have their ears tickled and the Word delivered to them in a manner they prefer.

So how does a new believer find a good Bible? Many new believers take recommendations from other Christians or from pastors and Bible teachers. If a person's heart is in the right place, and the Spirit of God dwells in them, they will eventually find the right Bible for themselves. But they must read and study it to be able to discern its value. I finally settled on the New American Standard Bible (1995) after many years of study. I started with the King James version, then went to the New King James version. Then, after Bible college and some seminary, I finally chose the New American Standard version for my personal study and for teaching. I have found it to be a highly reliable interpretation of the Greek, Aramaic and Hebrew manuscripts used to compile the Bible. It is best for me. You must find which is best for you.

The foundation for the need for God's Word as our lamp to guide our feet and to light our path must be firmly established. When Jesus was trying to encourage His disciples, He spoke these revealing and comforting words:

> Jesus answered and said to him, "If anyone loves Me, he will keep My word; and My Father will love him, and We will come to him and make Our abode with him. He who does not love Me does not keep My words; and the word which you hear is not Mine, but the Father's who sent Me.
>
> "These things I have spoken to you while abiding with you. But the Helper, the Holy Spirit, whom the Father will send in My name, He will teach you all things, and bring to your remembrance all that I said to you."[16]

The promise of the Helper, the Holy Spirit, to teach us all things and to bring to remembrance God's Words simply

---

16. John 14:23–26.

means that Christians will have all the help they need to discern God's truth in His Word. Those who profess Christianity but who do not love God's Word do not love God. They may have an external shell that claims salvation, but once they cross that bridge into eternity they may find themselves wanting.

Many think that the truth is whatever they believe to be true. God's truth is the truth whether someone believes it or not. Not believing it does not make it less than true. God is truth. Truth is a constant in our universe, and remains so regardless of whether or not we believe it. Anything contrary to God's Word is hopeless. God has provided the weapons we need to survive in this world. As Christians, we are instructed to take up the full armor of God—armor He freely gives to His children. Armor is meant to protect a person from the onslaughts of the enemy. It is lifesaving. When Paul was writing to the Ephesians, he explained the armor of God:

> Finally, be strong in the Lord and in the strength of His might. Put on the full armor of God, so that you will be able to stand firm against the schemes of the devil. For our struggle is not against flesh and blood, but against the rulers, against the powers, against the world forces of this darkness, against the spiritual forces of wickedness in the heavenly places. Therefore, take up the full armor of God, so that you will be able to resist in the evil day, and having done everything,

to stand firm. Stand firm therefore, HAVING GIRDED YOUR LOINS WITH TRUTH, and HAVING PUT ON THE BREASTPLATE OF RIGHTEOUSNESS, and having shod YOUR FEET WITH THE PREPARATION OF THE GOSPEL OF PEACE; in addition to all, taking up the shield of faith with which you will be able to extinguish all the flaming arrows of the evil one. And take THE HELMET OF SALVATION, and the sword of the Spirit, which is the word of God.[17]

The primary purpose of the full armor of God is, "so that you will be able to stand firm against the schemes of the devil." The master deceiver has an abundance of schemes, all designed to thwart God's Word and to enslave the masses. God's reason for providing us His armor is to protect us from the attacks of the devil, not from other people. The devil uses people to carry out his ungodly destruction, but our battle is not with people; it is with the devil and his minions. Paul says that "our struggle is not against flesh and blood, but against the rulers, against the powers, against the world forces of this darkness, against the spiritual forces of wickedness in the heavenly places." This is insightful when we strive to fully understand what is going on in our world. The battle is between God and Satan. Satan uses his puppets to attack God's Word and to attack God's people. Everything counter to God's Word

---

17. Ephesians 6:10–17. Words in all capitals are quotations from the Old Testament.

is an attempt at tearing the Lord's children down. Many succumb to the works of the devil simply because they do not know the Word of God. Others succumb because they would rather live in what appears to be a more fitting reality for themselves and refuse to embrace God's Word.

So stand firm! Know the truth in righteousness, know the gospel, and take up the shield of faith, which can extinguish the arrows of Satan. Take the helmet of salvation, having worked your salvation, and wield the sword, God's Word, truth! The interesting thing about a sword is that it is both an offensive and a defensive weapon. It is the most versatile and powerful weapon a person can have when battling the deception and schemes of the devil. We must know God's Word!

If even Jesus used Scripture to combat the enemy's arrows, how much more should we know Scripture to do the same!

> And the tempter came and said to Him, "If You are the Son of God, command that these stones become bread." But He answered and said, "*It is written*, 'MAN SHALL NOT LIVE ON BREAD ALONE, BUT ON EVERY WORD THAT PROCEEDS OUT OF THE MOUTH OF GOD.'"

> Then the devil took Him into the holy city and had Him stand on the pinnacle of the temple, and said to Him, "If You are the Son of God, throw Yourself down; for it is written,

> 'HE WILL COMMAND HIS ANGELS CONCERNING YOU';
>
> and
>
> 'ON their HANDS THEY WILL BEAR YOU UP,
>
> SO THAT YOU WILL NOT STRIKE YOUR FOOT AGAINST A STONE.'"
>
> Jesus said to him, "On the other hand, *it is written*, 'YOU SHALL NOT PUT THE LORD YOUR GOD TO THE TEST.'"
>
> Again, the devil took Him to a very high mountain and showed Him all the kingdoms of the world and their glory; and he said to Him, "All these things I will give You, if You fall down and worship me." Then Jesus said to him, "Go, Satan! *For it is written*, 'YOU SHALL WORSHIP THE LORD YOUR GOD, AND SERVE HIM ONLY.'" Then the devil left Him; and behold, angels came and began to minister to Him.[18]

Faith is essential in being able to distinguish the truth. People cannot discern, know, or fully understand God's Word

---

18. Matthew 4:3–11. Words in all capitals are quotations from the Old Testament. Emphasis mine.

without faith. Paul explains what this means in his first letter to the Corinthians:

> For to us God revealed them through the Spirit; for the Spirit searches all things, even the depths of God. For who among men knows the thoughts of a man except the spirit of the man which is in him? Even so the thoughts of God no one knows except the Spirit of God. *Now we have received, not the spirit of the world, but the Spirit who is from God, so that we may know the things freely given to us by God*, which things we also speak, not in words taught by human wisdom, but in those taught by the Spirit, combining spiritual thoughts with spiritual words.
>
> *But a natural man does not accept the things of the Spirit of God, for they are foolishness to him; and he cannot understand them, because they are spiritually appraised.* But he who is spiritual appraises all things, yet he himself is appraised by no one. For WHO HAS KNOWN THE MIND OF THE LORD, THAT HE WILL INSTRUCT HIM? But we have the mind of Christ.[19]

It is important that we understand this message. Anyone who thinks that the Word of God is foolishness is not of God.

---

[19]. 1 Corinthians 2:10–16. Words in all capitals are quotations from the Old Testament. Emphasis mine.

This person is still of the flesh: not born again of the Spirit of God. Anyone who does not embrace and love the Word of God is not of God. There is no convincing anyone unless God imparts to them the gift of faith. Faith is what enables one to see and know the things of God. Without the gift of faith, we are destined for outer darkness. A person cannot claim to be a Christian and not wholeheartedly embrace all of God's Word. They may think they are, but live only in an fake reality created by the enemy. Paul confirms this when writing to Timothy:

> Now you followed my teaching, conduct, purpose, faith, patience, love, perseverance, persecutions, and sufferings, such as happened to me at Antioch, at Iconium and at Lystra; what persecutions I endured, and out of them all the Lord rescued me! Indeed, all who desire to live godly in Christ Jesus will be persecuted. But evil men and impostors will proceed from bad to worse, deceiving and being deceived. *You, however, continue in the things you have learned and become convinced of, knowing from whom you have learned them, and that from childhood you have known the sacred writings which are able to give you the wisdom that leads to salvation through faith which is in Christ Jesus. All Scripture is inspired by God and profitable for teaching, for reproof, for correction, for training*

> *in righteousness; so that the man of God may be adequate, equipped for every good work.*[20]

The Word of God equips us for battle against the devil and his soldiers. The Word of God is essential to being on solid ground and being deeply rooted so that we can stand firm in this life.

---

20. 2 Timothy 3:10–16. Emphasis mine.

6

SALVATION

She will bear a Son; and you shall call His name Jesus, for He will save His people from their sins.

MATTHEW 1:21.

There are only two options in eternity: heaven or hell. Salvation is much more than an escape route from outer darkness. It is a priceless gift from our loving Father. Christians experience salvation in different ways but the result is the same: we become new creations, born again of the Spirit of God. There are no man-made formulas for salvation. No magic rituals, baptisms, spells, or incantations will ever result in a person being born again. Salvation is spiritual. It is not self-directed. It may be difficult to understand some things about the salvation process, and some may balk at the biblical teachings behind being saved. Denying God's Word will not suddenly make it untrue. The born-again person, possessed of the Spirit of God, will realize all of this as it unfolds. The natural person, devoid of the Spirit of God will only see it as foolishness.

We should never lose sight of the fact that the enemy is out to destroy God's children. He wants to keep us from the Father by twisting and transforming the Word of God into something more acceptable, more comforting, and less challenging. Being a Christian is being Christlike in a fallen world. There are no fancy receptions, awards, or acknowledgments in this life. The Christian's reward is realized only in heaven. Ours can be a very lonely and difficult experience. Throughout history the persecution of Christians has been extensive and brutal. At times it is much easier not to be a Christian, but salvation sets us apart from the rest of humanity.

Again, salvation is a gift. It can never be fabricated by people according to their own will. No one can decide to be saved and then be saved. The gift of salvation is of God alone and given according to His will. There are no altar calls or invitations that can command salvation to occur. Satan makes it appear as if we are in control of being born again but we are not. "Say this prayer, invite Jesus into your heart, kneel and confess your sins and be saved!" This is not how it works. Satan distorts the truth of salvation and many walk through life unchanged, unburdened, but thinking they are saved. If we have any real interest in salvation, or in the title of Christian, we must confirm our salvation. Once again remember the words of Paul the apostle, "So then, my beloved, just as you have always obeyed, not as in my presence only, but now much more in my absence, *work out your salvation with fear and trembling*; for it is God who is at work in you, both to will and to work for His good pleasure."[21]

---

21. Philippians 2:12–13. Emphasis mine.

In experience salvation is simple. It just happens. Remember the thief on the cross? Jesus told him, "Truly I say to you, today you will be with Me in paradise."[22] No altar call, no rote sayings, just belief exhibited by a person born again of the Spirit of God. A true believer expressing their faith in belief, a person able to see the truth. A person cannot truly believe without the gift of faith. *Faith is what enables belief* and understanding. No one can simply choose to see the things of God on a spiritual level without being enabled to do so by faith. First comes the gift of faith, then belief, and then salvation.

Paul says to the Ephesians:

> And you were dead in your trespasses and sins, in which you formerly walked according to the course of this world, according to the prince of the power of the air, of the spirit that is now working in the sons of disobedience. Among them we too all formerly lived in the lusts of our flesh, indulging the desires of the flesh and of the mind, and were by nature children of wrath, even as the rest. But God, being rich in mercy, because of His great love with which He loved us, even when we were dead in our transgressions, made us alive together with Christ (by grace you have been saved), and raised us up with Him, and seated us with Him

---

22. Luke 23:43.

> in the heavenly places in Christ Jesus, so that in the ages to come He might show the surpassing riches of His grace in kindness toward us in Christ Jesus. *For by grace you have been saved through faith; and that not of yourselves, it is the gift of God; not as a result of works, so that no one may boast.* For we are His workmanship, created in Christ Jesus for good works, which God prepared beforehand so that we would walk in them.[23]

The key statement "For by grace you have been saved through faith; and that not of yourselves, it is the gift of God; not as a result of works, so that no one may boast" states the reality of salvation clearly. Christians believe *because* they have been given the gift of faith and have been born again of the Spirit of God. They have been transformed from being a creature of the old nature into one with a new nature, to be a spiritual child of God. Nicodemus, a Jewish teacher and Pharisee was confused about Jesus, who He was and for what purpose He had come. This is the discussion Jesus had with Nicodemus:

> Now there was a man of the Pharisees, named Nicodemus, a ruler of the Jews; this man came to Jesus by night and said to Him, "Rabbi, we know that You have come from God as a teacher; for no one can do these signs that You do unless God is with him." Jesus answered and said to him,

---

23. Ephesians 2:1–10. Emphasis mine.

Salvation

"Truly, truly, I say to you, unless one is born again, he cannot see the kingdom of God."

Nicodemus said to Him, "How can a man be born when he is old? He cannot enter a second time into his mother's womb and be born, can he?" Jesus answered, "Truly, truly, I say to you, unless one is born of water and the Spirit he cannot enter into the kingdom of God. That which is born of the flesh is flesh, and that which is born of the Spirit is spirit. Do not be amazed that I said to you, 'You must be born again.' The wind blows where it wishes and you hear the sound of it, but do not know where it comes from and where it is going; so is everyone who is born of the Spirit."

Nicodemus said to Him, "How can these things be?" Jesus answered and said to him, "Are you the teacher of Israel and do not understand these things? Truly, truly, I say to you, we speak of what we know and testify of what we have seen, and you do not accept our testimony. If I told you earthly things and you do not believe, how will you believe if I tell you heavenly things? No one has ascended into heaven, but He who descended from heaven: the Son of Man. As Moses lifted up the serpent in the wilderness, even so must the Son of Man be lifted up; so that whoever believes will in Him have eternal life.

> "For God so loved the world, that He gave His only begotten Son, that whoever believes in Him shall not perish, but have eternal life. For God did not send the Son into the world to judge the world, but that the world might be saved through Him. He who believes in Him is not judged; he who does not believe has been judged already, because he has not believed in the name of the only begotten Son of God. This is the judgment, that the Light has come into the world, and men loved the darkness rather than the Light, for their deeds were evil. For everyone who does evil hates the Light and does not come to the Light for fear that his deeds will be exposed. But he who practices the truth comes to the Light, so that his deeds may be manifested as having been wrought in God."[24]

This is a discussion Jesus is having with a well-educated Jewish scholar, a teacher of the Jewish law, a man who would be comparable today to one of our professors with a doctorate in theology. Nicodemus simply could not understand the concept of being born again of the Spirit of God. If we believe that Jesus is the Christ, the Son of God, then there is strong evidence that we may be born again. Jesus came to earth, took on flesh, and was crucified and put to death to make salvation possible. The cost was astronomical and the benefits to those who believe, immeasurable. Being born

---

24. John 3:1–23.

again is evidenced by a transformation from one nature to another, from being a natural person to becoming a child of God, possessed of His Spirit. It is a transformation from being unable to see or understand the reality of God, to seeing, understanding, embracing, and loving it.

> THE WORD IS NEAR YOU, IN YOUR MOUTH AND IN YOUR HEART"—that is, the word of faith which we are preaching, that if you confess with your mouth Jesus as Lord, and believe in your heart that God raised Him from the dead, you will be saved; for with the heart a person believes, resulting in righteousness, and with the mouth he confesses, resulting in salvation. For the Scripture says, "WHOEVER BELIEVES IN HIM WILL NOT BE DISAPPOINTED." For there is no distinction between Jew and Greek; for the same Lord is Lord of all, abounding in riches for all who call on Him; for "WHOEVER WILL CALL ON THE NAME OF THE LORD WILL BE SAVED.[25]

The key, the enabler, is the gift of faith. When that gift is given, belief becomes possible through hearing the Word of God. It causes the new birth. We are forever changed:

> But we should always give thanks to God for you, brethren beloved by the Lord, *because God has*

---

25. Romans 10:8–13. Words in all capitals are quotations from the Old Testament.

> *chosen you from the beginning for salvation through sanctification by the Spirit and faith in the truth. It was for this He called you through our gospel*, that you may gain the glory of our Lord Jesus Christ. So then, brethren, stand firm and hold to the traditions which you were taught, whether by word of mouth or by letter from us.[26]

Salvation does not occur without dramatic changes to our personalities: "Therefore, if anyone is in Christ, he is a new creature; the old things passed away; behold, new things have come."[27] We hear hundreds of testimonies from Christians. Many speak of their "experience." The saving event may be an experience to some and not so much to others. Aligning our experience with someone else's may not be profitable. Remember the parable of the sower. Different levels of experience and changes take place in all four examples:

> Hear then the parable of the sower. *When anyone hears the word of the kingdom and does not understand it, the evil one comes and snatches away what has been sown in his heart.* This is the one on whom seed was sown beside the road. The one on whom seed was sown on the rocky places, this is the man who hears the word and immediately receives it with joy; yet he has no firm

---

26. 2 Thessalonians 2:13–15. Emphasis mine.

27. 2 Corinthians 5:17.

root in himself, but is only temporary, *and when affliction or persecution arises because of the word, immediately he falls away.* And the one on whom seed was sown among the thorns, this is the man who hears the word, *and the worry of the world and the deceitfulness of wealth choke the word, and it becomes unfruitful.* And the one on whom seed was sown on the good soil, *this is the man who hears the word and understands it*; who indeed bears fruit and brings forth, some a hundredfold, some sixty, and some thirty.[28]

Three of the four categories were false starts. Affliction, persecution, worries of this life, the deceitfulness of wealth all brings the initial hearing and reactions to nothing. When God provides the gift of faith, the presence of the Holy Spirit within us enables us to persevere in God's will. Perfectly? No. But He helps us to be continuously cognizant and willing. The fact that many are called but few chosen is important to remember. The road to eternal life is narrow and the road to destruction wide, and many are those who go by the wide road. Satan works constantly at making the wide road more desirable. He works overtime throwing obstacles in our path to disrupt our journey, and to cast doubt. Born-again Christians have the Holy Spirit within them to teach them God's Word and to give them strength to persevere in the most

---

28. Matthew 13:18–23. Emphasis mine.

difficult of times. It is disheartening to see that so many who claim to be Christians may fall short of being saved.

No one can save themselves. No one can say, "I am saved because I asked Jesus into my heart," or because, "I accepted Jesus as my Lord and Savior." Who are we that we can move the hand of God to provide such an eternal gift, thinking we are empowered to save ourselves from sin and eternal death? Think of what that would really mean. "I said this" or "I did that and saved myself." "I moved the hand of God." Many just accept things blindly because it sounds good, or it is easy, or because they are temporarily enthralled with the speaker. These people may perish because of their ignorance and lack of love for the truth.

> Jesus says, "*No one can come to Me unless the Father who sent Me draws him*; and I will raise him up on the last day."[29]

> Jesus says, "I am the way, and the truth, and the life; *no one comes to the Father but through Me.*"[30]

> Paul says, "*For by grace, you have been saved through faith; and that not of yourselves, it is the gift of God; not as a result of works, so that no one may boast.* For we are His workmanship, created in Christ

---

29. John 6:44. Emphasis mine.

30. John 14:6. Emphasis mine.

> Jesus for good works, which God prepared beforehand so that we would walk in them."[31]

> Paul says, *"On the contrary, who are you, O man, who answers back to God? The thing molded will not say to the molder, "Why did you make me like this," will it?* Or does not the potter have a right over the clay, to make from the same lump one vessel for honorable use and another for common use?"[32]

Remember, we did not choose to be fearfully and wonderfully made and born of the flesh from the womb of our mothers. It was a miracle of life given by God. That is the beauty of being saved, knowing that God chose us because He loved us before He even created the foundations of the world. We love Him *only* because He first loved us.

> Now the word of the LORD came to Jeremiah saying, "Before I formed you in the womb I knew you, and before you were born, I consecrated you."[33]

Being born again means we are new creations, possessing the new nature of Christ within our fleshly bodies, meaning a new and lifelong battle between our new and old nature.

---

31. Ephesians 2:8–10. Emphasis mine.
32. Romans 9:20–21.
33. Jeremiah 1:4–5.

The transformation may be different for each person, but the result is always the same: Christlikeness. It's like the metamorphosis of the once grounded, leaf-eating caterpillars that turn into beautiful, free butterflies, enjoying the nectar of sweet flowers while soaring high above their past life. They enjoy a new perspective of their world and are equipped differently. They can see far beyond the minimal perspective they had in their old life. So it is with the born-again Christian. A new life. A new perspective. New equipment. Boundless new possibilities.

If these attributes are missing, so too may salvation be missing. From the point of our new birth, we will be challenged and tested. Peter summed it up wonderfully:

> Blessed be the God and Father of our Lord Jesus Christ, *who according to His great mercy has caused us to be born again* to a living hope through the resurrection of Jesus Christ from the dead, to obtain an inheritance which is imperishable and undefiled and will not fade away, reserved in heaven for you, *who are protected by the power of God through faith for a salvation ready to be revealed in the last time*. In this you greatly rejoice, even though now for a little while, if necessary, you have been distressed by various trials, so that the proof of your faith, being more precious than gold which is perishable, even though tested by fire, may be found to result in praise and glory

and honor at the revelation of Jesus Christ; and though you have not seen Him, you love Him, and though you do not see Him now, but believe in Him, you greatly rejoice with joy inexpressible and full of glory, *obtaining as the outcome of your faith the salvation of your souls*. As to this salvation, the prophets who prophesied of the grace that would come to you made careful searches and inquiries, seeking to know what person or time the Spirit of Christ within them was indicating as He predicted the sufferings of Christ and the glories to follow. It was revealed to them that they were not serving themselves, but you, in these things which now have been announced to you through those who preached the gospel to you by the Holy Spirit sent from heaven—things into which angels long to look.[34]

Peter sums up the entire process and helps us to understand that our faith is so valuable that we will be tested to help us know it is real. But understand that these various trails of our faith will also reveal those who make false claims and are not born again. These trials occur repeatedly during our lifetime—sometimes even daily. In our current world believers are constantly being bombarded by the arrows of Satan. Just look at what the world at large wants everyone to believe and embrace, and those not well equipped to fight will find

---

34. 1 Peter 1:3–12. Emphasis mine.

themselves overwhelmed. How we live in this world paints an accurate picture of the true state of our conversion. We will in a sense be visible as Christ to the world and not as our old selves, having forsaken the old nature for our new one. If this does not describe us, we may not be saved. The same holds true when we consider the church of Jesus Christ.

7

THE CHURCH

To me, the very least of all saints, this grace was given, to preach to the Gentiles the unfathomable riches of Christ, and to bring to light what is the administration of the mystery which for ages has been hidden in God who created all things; so that the manifold wisdom of God might now be made known through the church to the rulers and the authorities in the heavenly places.

EPHESIANS 3:8–10

We are the church of Jesus Christ. Those things we call "churches" are buildings built by men. Satan has destroyed the concept of the church. The visible church has acquiesced to Satan's deceptions over the years and looks nothing like the original church of Jesus' followers. Like many professing to be Christians, but who are not, much of the visible church professes to be of Christ and is not. Possession of the Spirit of God and the knowledge of His Word are critical to our understanding of what is happening in our world. We, the born-again believers, are the church. The devil has succeeded in having us externalize the internal reality of the born-again believers being the church. Church has now become somewhere we go. It is a building. We must begin to see and to understand just how much the devil has twisted God's reality and we must realign ourselves with God's word, find the truth, and stand determined in it.

When John wrote to the seven churches in the book of Revelation, he was writing to the called-out ones, the believers, in Thessalonica, Ephesus, Thyatira, Philadelphia, Laodicea, Pergamum, Smyrna, and Sardis. He was not writing to the Baptists, Methodists, Catholics, or Lutherans. The Christian church has evolved over the centuries into a dysfunctional and divisive entity we now call the visible church. The same negative evolution has occurred within Christianity and what it means to be a Christian. Paul rebuked the Corinthians for their divisiveness but not before exclaiming who they were in Christ:

> Paul, called as an apostle of Jesus Christ by the will of God, and Sosthenes our brother, *To the church of God*, which is at Corinth, to those who have been sanctified in Christ Jesus, *saints by calling*, with all who in every place call on the name of our Lord Jesus Christ, their Lord and ours:
>
> Grace to you and peace from God our Father and the Lord Jesus Christ.
>
> I thank my God always concerning you for the grace of God which was given you in Christ Jesus, that in everything you were enriched in Him, in all speech and all knowledge, even as the testimony concerning Christ was confirmed in you, so that you are not lacking in any gift, awaiting eagerly the revelation of our Lord Jesus Christ, who will also confirm you to the end, blameless in the day of our Lord Jesus Christ. *God is faithful,*

*through whom you were called into fellowship with
His Son, Jesus Christ our Lord.*[35]

Humankind, in its shortsightedness, destroys everything it takes control over. It pilfers, commands, imprisons, and controls to its own earthly benefit. What has happened to the church is no different. The modern church is the work of man. This is why knowledge of God's Word is essential. Repeatedly confronted with God's reality, we will begin to see that the visible church and modern, pop Christianity, is a dangerous facade that entraps many of the unsuspecting. Paul says to the Thessalonians:

> For the mystery of lawlessness is already at work; only he who now restrains will do so until he is taken out of the way. Then that lawless one will be revealed whom the Lord will slay with the breath of His mouth and bring to an end by the appearance of His coming; that is, the one whose coming is in accord with the activity of Satan, with all power and signs and false wonders, *and with all the deception of wickedness for those who perish, because they did not receive the love of the truth so as to be saved.*[36]

It cannot be said any plainer than this: people are going to

---

35. 1 Corinthians 1:1–9. Emphasis mine.

36. 2 Thessalonians 2:7–10. Emphasis mine.

perish because they did not receive the love of the truth to be saved. Without the truth we cannot evaluate and test the things put before us. We can easily be deceived. But if we love the truth, seek it out, embrace it, use it as the true standard by which we assess ourselves and the world, we will be saved from what is to come. The church is the body of Christ, His bride. Its purpose is to grow into a mature singularity, a mature man as Paul puts it to the Ephesians:

> In Him, you also, after listening to the message of truth, the gospel of your salvation—having also believed, you were sealed in Him with the Holy Spirit of promise, who is given as a pledge of our inheritance, with a view to the redemption of God's own possession, to the praise of His glory. For this reason, I too, having heard of the faith in the Lord Jesus which exists among you and your love for all the saints, do not cease giving thanks for you, while making mention of you in my prayers; *that the God of our Lord Jesus Christ, the Father of glory, may give to you a spirit of wisdom and of revelation in the knowledge of Him.* I pray that the eyes of your heart may be enlightened, so that you will know what is the hope of His calling, what are the riches of the glory of His inheritance in the saints, and what is the surpassing greatness of His power toward us who believe. These are in accordance with the working of the strength of His might which He brought

about in Christ, when He raised Him from the dead and seated Him at His right hand in the heavenly places, far above all rule and authority and power and dominion, and every name that is named, not only in this age but also in the one to come. And He put all things in subjection under His feet and gave Him as head over all things to the church, which is His body, the fullness of Him who fills all in all.[37]

To me, the very least of all saints, this grace was given, to preach to the Gentiles the unfathomable riches of Christ, and to bring to light what is the administration of the mystery which for ages has been hidden in God who created all things; *so that the manifold wisdom of God might now be made known through the church to the rulers and the authorities in the heavenly places.*[38]

And He gave some as apostles, and some as prophets, and some as evangelists, and some as pastors and teachers, for the equipping of the saints for the work of service, *to the building up of the body of Christ; until we all attain to the unity of the faith, and of the knowledge of the Son of God, to a mature man, to the measure of the stature which belongs to*

---

37. Ephesians 1:13, 23.

38. Ephesians 3:8–10. Emphasis mine.

> *the fullness of Christ.* As a result, we are no longer to be children, tossed here and there by waves and carried about by every wind of doctrine, by the trickery of men, by craftiness in deceitful scheming; but speaking the truth in love, we are to grow up in all aspects into Him who is the head, even Christ, from whom the whole body, being fitted and held together by what every joint supplies, according to the proper working of each individual part, causes the growth of the body for the building up of itself in love.[39]

The body of Christ, His church, has one primary mission: *to be unified into a single body.* God provides teachers, pastors, and others

> for the equipping of the saints for the work of service, to the building up of the body of Christ; until we all attain to the unity of the faith, and of the knowledge of the Son of God, to a mature man, to the measure of the stature which belongs to the fullness of Christ. [40]

Specifically, Paul warns us that the enemy of this progression is ignorance of the truth, which causes us to be carried about by endless, but attractive, false doctrines, engineered

---

39. Ephesians 4:11–16.

40. Ephesians 4:12-13.

by crafty and deceitful men led by Satan to trick the believer into a false understanding, and away from God the Father.

The visible church has failed miserably at protecting and keeping the Word of God as its sole foundation. It's primary purpose, again, is

> speaking the truth in love, we are to grow up in all aspects into Him who is the head, even Christ, from whom the whole body, being fitted and held together by what every joint supplies, according to the proper working of each individual part, causes the growth of the body for the building up of itself in love.[41]

Acknowledging that Jesus Christ is the head of the church, the body, is to be fitted and held together—*unified*—by what every joint supplies, according to the proper working of each part, causing the growth of the body for the building up of itself in love! So why do we have so many Christian denominations across the world? This is the antithesis of what the Father intended for the church of Jesus Christ. This is an abomination that most professing Christians are not even cognizant exists right before our eyes. But the question is, why does it continue to flourish? Satan has captured the minds and hearts of so many, appearing to be an angel of light, a wolf in sheep's clothing. This deliberate distortion of God's plan for His church began shortly after Jesus' resurrection.

---

41. Ephesian 4:15-16.

Paul addresses this issue as it is occurring in the church at Corinth:

> Now I exhort you, brethren, by the name of our Lord Jesus Christ, *that you all agree and that there be no divisions among you, but that you be made complete in the same mind and in the same judgment.* For I have been informed concerning you, my brethren, by Chloe's people, that there are quarrels among you. *Now I mean this, that each one of you is saying, "I am of Paul," and "I of Apollos," and "I of Cephas," and "I of Christ." Has Christ been divided?* Paul was not crucified for you, was he? Or were you baptized in the name of Paul? I thank God that I baptized none of you except Crispus and Gaius, so that no one would say you were baptized in my name.[42]

This is the modern-day equivalent of saying, "I am a Baptist or Lutheran or Catholic or Methodist" or any other "thing" created out of the mind of men. There are numerous excuses, but none will exonerate us on judgment day. "But I did not know" will be a futile defense, because every one of us has the tools to discover the truth. Just look at the modern visible church system. It mandates pastors to be seminary graduates, "churchgoers" to become official members, and all to profess allegiance to their creed. Where is any of that in the Word of

---

42. 1 Corinthians 1:10–15. Emphasis mine.

God? It does not exist. It is divisive. We have chopped up the body of Christ through disagreements and ignorance. How can any men, allegedly called to lead God's children as pastors or teachers, repeat the same grievous errors Paul addressed nearly two thousand years ago? By doing so they perpetuate division in the body of Christ. The visible church is not the body of Jesus Christ. It is a distraction from the enemy:

> *For even as the body is one and yet has many members, and all the members of the body, though they are many, are one body, so also is Christ.* For by one Spirit we were all baptized into *one body*, whether Jews or Greeks, whether slaves or free, and we were all made to drink of one Spirit.
>
> For the body is not one member, but many. If the foot says, "Because I am not a hand, I am not a part of the body," it is not for this reason any the less a part of the body. And if the ear says, "Because I am not an eye, I am not a part of the body," it is not for this reason any the less a part of the body. If the whole body were an eye, where would the hearing be? If the whole were hearing, where would the sense of smell be? But now God has placed the members, each one of them, in the body, just as He desired. If they were all one member, where would the body be? *But now there are many members, but one body*. And the eye cannot say to the hand, "I have no need

of you"; or again the head to the feet, "I have no need of you." On the contrary, it is much truer that the members of the body which seem to be weaker are necessary; and those members of the body which we deem less honorable, on these we bestow more abundant honor, and our less presentable members become much more presentable, whereas our more presentable members have no need of it. But God has so composed the body, giving more abundant honor to that member which lacked, *so that there may be no division in the body*, but that the members may have the same care for one another. And if one member suffers, all the members suffer with it; if one member is honored, all the members rejoice with it.

Now you are Christ's body, and individually members of it.[43]

This does not mean that the visible church is devoid of born-again Christians or that they are all led by evil men. Remember Jesus' words "If anyone wants to be first, he shall be last of all and servant of all."[44] So why name a church "First Baptist" or "Second Presbyterian"? How can any denomination continue after reading what Paul wrote to the Corinthians

---

43. 1 Corinthians 12:12–27. Emphasis mine.

44. Mark 9:35.

and to the Ephesians? Can anyone picture Jesus, the Head of His church, wearing a golden ephod and gold jewelry, sitting in a palace surrounded by priceless art and making His followers kiss His ring? Jesus was our model for the Christian life and the model for our church leaders. If you do not see Christ, you do not see the Spirit of God.

Why are there so many denominations? What sets them apart from each other? They believe differently. A discord arose over some, and in many cases incredibly minor, theological point and they divided. Then they divided again, and again, and again. So, it was not Christlikeness or unity as the primary purpose: it was differences and division. Again, the antithesis of what Scripture teaches. How did we fall so far from the truth? It is so much easier to just maintain the status quo than be bothered with knowing the Word of God, and then challenging the deception. The enemy likes us ignorant. Ignorance is bliss up and until that final day.

There have been many good and faithful pastors and teachers who have attempted to move away from division and the self-proclaiming of a denominational title and all the politics that go along with any human-caused system. They generally consider themselves to be nondenominational. Many have moved out and planted fellowships only to be overcome by fleshly systemics and setting up a board of directors, paying homage to the Federal Government by gaining tax exemption status, building huge complexes and leading quiet and easy lives. Jesus says, "Then render to Caesar the things that are Caesar's; and to God the things that are God's."[45]

Every fellowship that partners with the government of men by becoming a human-caused not-for-profit organization to gain tax exemptions has sold its pulpit. They have exchanged the freedom of teaching God's Word for monetary gain. They have softened the edges of God's Word to maintain a viable, human-caused entity. Was God not able to provide for them without them selling their freedom for a tax exemption?

Others understood the truth and God gathered around them His children and a fellowship of Christian believers formed and they studied and learned the Word of God together. When we read church history, it is interesting to learn that those whom history considers to be some of the greatest teachers and pastors began their ministries in the organized visible church, but when they found the truth in God's Word and began to teach it, they were ostracized and became outcasts. The Word of God is sharper than a two-edged sword, and it cuts to the quick. It comes down to this: if you really want to know the truth it is easy to find. But finding the right fellowship will take effort and patience.

Christianity has nothing to do with which fellowship we call home. Christianity is a simple reality that begins once

---

45. Matthew 22:21.

we are born again and equipped with the Spirit of God who will lead us into all truth:

> These things I have spoken to you while abiding with you. But the Helper, the Holy Spirit, whom the Father will send in My name, *He will teach you all things*, and bring to your remembrance all that I said to you.[46]

The real question here is, do we really *want* to know the truth? The world God created crucified Jesus. He came to His own and His own rejected Him. Why? What did Jesus do to deserve crucifixion? If we read the Gospels again and try to find out who Jesus really was, what He did, and what He said, we will not find a legitimate reason to kill Him. But they did. They brought false witnesses against Him. They enraged the public with exaggerations and lies to make them fearful. They riled up the crowd to scream for His crucifixion and the release of a murderer. The reasons they killed Him were self-preserving. They believed that He threatened their status, their comfort, their way of life.

What do we do with the modern visible church and those who profess Christianity but do not seek the truth? We teach them with all gentleness and patience, exhorting and correcting with the Word of God. We pray for them. But in the end, all that can be said of those who do not heed the truth is what Jesus says regarding the teachers of Israel:

---

46. John 14:25–26. Emphasis mine.

> Then the disciples came and said to Him, "Do You know that the Pharisees were offended when they heard this statement?" But He answered and said, "Every plant which My heavenly Father did not plant shall be uprooted. Let them alone; they are blind guides of the blind. And if a blind man guides a blind man, both will fall into a pit."[47]

The shame in all of this is that there are many well-intentioned teachers, pastors, and followers. There are many places to get solid biblical teaching up to a point but there is no perfect fellowship. In the end, if we diligently read the Scriptures we will eventually be confronted with a truth we do not currently embrace. That is the test of a lifetime. What will we do when after years of superficial acceptance and meager effort, we finally come face to face with God's Word and realize we are not following it?

Friendship with the world is enmity toward God. The world will hate you as it hated Jesus. In this world you will have tribulation. The question is will we repent, pick up that cross, and follow Him, regardless of the cost?

---

47. Mathew 15:12–14.

8

THE WORLD

You lust and do not have; so you commit murder. You are envious and cannot obtain; so you fight and quarrel. You do not have because you do not ask. You ask and do not receive, because you ask with wrong motives, so that you may spend it on your pleasures. You adulteresses, do you not know that friendship with the world is hostility toward God? Therefore whoever wishes to be a friend of the world makes himself an enemy of God.

JAMES 4:2–4

Finally, we arrive at the universal testing ground where our faith is tried. We live in a world created by God the Father, where sin has crept in over thousands of years and taken control. There is no better mirror to reflect the condition of our souls than our relationship with the world and the people in it. We are each given our lifetimes to work out our salvation and a sinful world to reflect the state of our souls. If we are born again and the Spirit of God inhabits us, there is nothing more telling than our sometimes-mundane day-to-day experiences. If we take the time to slow down and peer into our daily routines, relationships, thoughts, words, and deeds, we will find a clearer answer to our salvation question.

It is telling that James says, "Do you not know that friendship with the world is hostility toward God? Therefore, whoever wishes to be a friend of the world makes himself an enemy of God."[48] Remember the parable of the sower: the cares of

---

48. James 4:4.

this world and the lust of riches corrupted the seed sown into so many hearts. Jesus says:

> "YOU SHALL LOVE THE LORD YOUR GOD WITH ALL YOUR HEART, AND WITH ALL YOUR SOUL, AND WITH ALL YOUR MIND. This is the great and foremost commandment. The second is like it, "YOU SHALL LOVE YOUR NEIGHBOR AS YOURSELF." On these two commandments depend the whole Law and the Prophets.[49]

Powerful and sobering words. The greatest proof of our salvation is our love for God the Father and our love toward our neighbors, but friendship with the world makes us an enemy of God.

Paul says, "Test yourselves to see if you are in the faith; examine yourselves! Or do you not recognize this about yourselves, that Jesus Christ is in you—unless indeed you fail the test?"[50] How do we evaluate ourselves? We look in the mirror the Word provides. It is right in front of us every day. It seems plain enough: love the Father with all our heart, mind and soul, and our neighbor as ourselves. But what does that look like when played out in our daily routines? How do we interact with those around us? How do we brand ourselves,

---

49. Matthew 22:37–40.

50. 2 Corinthians 13:5. Words in all capitals are quotations from the Old Testament.

constantly comparing ourselves with others instead of Jesus, which labels do we embrace, which ones do we hate? Are our words, thoughts and deeds found acceptable by our Lord? How often do we walk side by side with Jesus as we stroll through our daily lives? Are God's pleasure and will our primary motives in life? Are we one mind, one body? Are we seeking His will or our own?

Paul helps us to better understand the fruit we produce when we possess the Spirit of God:

> But the fruit of the Spirit is love, joy, peace, patience, kindness, goodness, faithfulness, gentleness, self-control; against such things there is no law. *Now those who belong to Christ Jesus have crucified the flesh with its passions and desires.*
>
> *If we live by the Spirit, let us also walk by the Spirit. Let us not become boastful, challenging one another, envying one another.*[51]

As believers we are called to be the light of the world, reflecting the love and will of God the Father and our Lord and Savior Jesus Christ. Boldness has disappeared in many parts of the world. Darkness is smothering the light. And it has been occurring at a much more rapid pace in the past few decades.

---

51. Galatians 5:22–26. Emphasis Mine.

The reality of this fallen world and the shadows that enshroud it are easily explainable. The constant dimming of the light and growing evil have been foretold. As the apostle Paul says:

> For the mystery of lawlessness is already at work; only he who now restrains will do so until he is taken out of the way. Then that lawless one will be revealed whom the Lord will slay with the breath of His mouth and bring to an end by the appearance of His coming; that is, the one whose coming is in accord with the activity of Satan, with all power and signs and false wonders, and with all the deception of wickedness for those who perish, because they did not receive the love of the truth so as to be saved. For this reason, God will send upon them a deluding influence so that they will believe what is false, in order that they all may be judged who did not believe the truth but took pleasure in wickedness.[52]

> But the Spirit explicitly says that in later times some will fall away from the faith, paying attention to deceitful spirits and doctrines of demons, by means of the hypocrisy of liars seared in their own conscience as with a branding iron, men who forbid marriage and advocate abstaining from foods which God has created to be gratefully shared in by

---

52. 2 Thessalonians 2:7–12.

> those who believe and know the truth. For everything created by God is good, and nothing is to be rejected if it is received with gratitude; for it is sanctified by means of the word of God and prayer.[53]

We who possess the Spirit of God can see this happening before our eyes. Those lacking the Spirit of God can neither see nor understand. There is a tremendous amount of insight in the words of Paul: a keen understanding of God's reality and Satan's false reality; a grasping of the destruction of God's Word, His church, and the falling away of millions as they become immersed in a fallen, sinful world. Being born again is the easy part—God does that. But living out our salvation in a sinful world is the hard part. It requires serious study and ongoing repentance. But love is the difference. The Greek word *agape* describes God's unconditional love, which we as Christians are meant to possess. They will know us by our love—our love of God the Father and our neighbor. This is what sets us apart from the fallen.

> Blessed is a man who perseveres under trial; for once he has been approved, he will receive the crown of life which the Lord has promised to those who love Him. Let no one say when he is tempted, "I am being tempted by God"; for God cannot be tempted by evil, and He Himself does not tempt anyone. But each one is tempted when

---

53. 2 Timothy 4:1–5.

> he is carried away and enticed by his own lust. Then when lust has conceived, it gives birth to sin; and when sin is accomplished, it brings forth death. Do not be deceived, my beloved brethren. Every good thing given and every perfect gift is from above, coming down from the Father of lights, with whom there is no variation or shifting shadow. In the exercise of His will He brought us forth by the word of truth, so that we would be a kind of first fruits among His creatures.[54]

It is easy to blame God but hard to blame ourselves. But all sin is the result of our choosing the wrong word, the wrong action, the wrong thoughts. It is sin and we are responsible for all of it. "But God could make it all so much easier!" So true! But then how would we ever know if we were truly saved? How could we be certain that our eternity would be spent with our Father in heaven? It is always easiest to blame the other person, or to blame God for not using His superpowers to clean up the world. We fail to understand that God *has* provided us a way out: "For God so loved the world, that He gave His only begotten Son, that whoever believes in Him shall not perish, but have eternal life."[55]

It all comes down to this: Are we being lights in this world? Does our love for God and our neighbor define us? Are we

---

54. James 1:12–18.

55. John 3:16.

lovers of God and His will? The world at large is not. It is evil and hates God, His purpose, and His people. Are we attuned to the enemy's relentless campaign against everything God holds dear? He wants to defile marriage, sex, family, and children. He has turned sex into perversion, marriage into a commodity, and children into sexual pawns. He uses quaint words such as "friends with benefits," "a casual affair," "freedom of reproductive rights," "tolerance, inclusion, and personal rights," hiding the dark reality of distortion and sin. He has taken the rainbow, a sign given to us by God as assurance that He would never again destroy the world with water, and made it a banner for what God calls sexual perversion (Please see Genesis 1:27; Leviticus 20:13; Matthew 19:5; Romans 1:26-27; 1 Corinthians 6:9-10). Under the disguise of compassion, compromise, and tolerance Satan pulls God's people away from abiding in His will. Millions have been misled by these tactics. The devil demands that his world embrace these perversions and celebrate them or be called out as bigots. This further weakens their resolve and hastens their destruction.

A born-again Christian cannot embrace or celebrate sin. Neither can we fail to embrace personal responsibility and truth. If we do, we cannot count ourselves as being saved. The difference should be stark—no mingling of light with darkness. We proudly embrace many labels publicly but inwardly cringe at the label of "Christian." The mirror provided by this world is well focused. We need to look into it and judge ourselves before that final judgment, which creeps closer to each of us every day. Remember when the Jewish leaders confronted Jesus after He had cast out the demons? They said that Jesus must be of Satan, using Satan's power to cast out the demons. Jesus said that was ridiculous: If He were of Satan, why would He be casting out Satan's demons? It made no sense. It would be a house divided against itself and would fall. The same holds true for those possessed by the Spirit of God! If we are truly Christians, then how can our thoughts, actions, associations, labels, or celebrations be in direct contradiction to God's? They cannot.

Jesus says:

> Therefore everyone who confesses Me before men, I will also confess him before My Father who is in heaven. But whoever denies Me before men, I will also deny him before My Father who is in heaven. Do not think that I came to bring peace on the earth; I did not come to bring peace, but a sword. For I came to SET A MAN AGAINST HIS FATHER, AND A DAUGHTER AGAINST HER MOTHER, AND A DAUGHTER-IN-LAW AGAINST HER MOTHER-IN-LAW; and A MAN'S ENEMIES WILL BE THE MEMBERS OF HIS HOUSEHOLD. He who loves father or mother more than Me is not worthy of Me; and he who loves son or daughter more than Me is not worthy of Me. And he who does not take his cross and follow after Me is not worthy of Me. He who has found his life

will lose it, and he who has lost his life for My sake will find it.[56]

We will have trials and tribulations in this life. We will have family, friends, and coworkers who embrace the ways of the fallen world. They will point us out as bigots; intolerant and uncompassionate. If we weaken and join them, we deny Jesus. The sheep versus the goats. *The last sermon.*

---

56. Matthew 10:32–39. Words in all capitals are quotations from the Old Testament.

Made in the USA
Middletown, DE
11 September 2024